Another Offering

SHAMA GANDHI

Another Offering

Published by:
Mata Amritanandamayi Mission Trust
Amritapuri P.O., Kollam Dt., Kerala
INDIA 690525
Email: info@theammashop.org
Website: www.amritapuri.org

Brahmārpanam brahma havir
Brahmāgnau brahmanāhutam;
Brahmaiva tena gantavyam
Brahma karma samādhinā

The act of offering is God (Brahma), the oblation is God, By God it is offered into the fire of God, God is That which is to be attained by him who sees God in all.

about

"*Another Offering*" is dedicated to celebrating Mata Amritanandamyi's (Amma) 65th birthday. With this book, I hope to inspire new cooks to experiment and make nutritious and wholesome home cooked meals as a gift of love, to nourish themselves, and their loved ones.

Thanks to my family for supporting all my endeavors. Thanks to award winning photographer Edwin Loyola for taking the beautiful pictures. Thanks to Amritashree for helping me to put the book together!

My eternal gratitude to our Amma who inspires us all to do selfless deeds, answers my prayers and sends me the right help in perfect time.

All the proceeds from this book will go to Amma's Embracing the World charities worldwide.

table of contents

table of contents

table of contents

RICE, GRAINS, AND BREADS (CONTINUED)

CHUTNEYS, DIPS, AND SPREADS 97

DESSERTS AND SWEET ENDINGS 109

table of contents

benefits of spices

Asafetida
Relieves gas pains, flatulence, a digestive agent

Basil
Good overall tonic for the nervous system

Bay Leaf
Carminative, stimulates and a good expectorant

Cardamom
Natural breath freshener, appetite stimulates and digestive aid

Cinnamon
Aids in digestion, good remedy for colds

Clove
Helps treating toothaches, relieves flatulence. Stimulates circulation, promotes digestion.

Cilantro
Natural digestive aid and expectorant

Cumin
Helps relieve nausea, aids digestion

Fennel
Cooling effect on the body, good digestive aid, tonifying for the stomach

Tamarind
Digestive aid with a cooling effect on the body

benefits of spices

Garlic
Helps relieve congestion, helps clear the arteries, and lower blood pressure

Ginger
Stimulates digestive aid. Helps in treating common cold and coughs

Mustard Seeds
Stimulates, expectorant and carminative

Curry Leaves
Cooling effect on the body and helps remove waste

Nutmeg
Digestive aid, helps in treating nausea

Onion
Stimulates and mild counter irritant. Natural diuretic. Helps remove catarrhal matter and phlegm from the bronchial tubes.

Pepper
Stimulates and digestive aid

Saffron
Cooling, a natural toning and digestive aid

Turmeric
Has cooling, cleansing, and detoxifying properties. It is also a natural antibacterial.

rx

Food is essential for creating and sustaining life. For optimal health, fresh cooked vegetarian food made with seasonal organic ingredients is revitalizing. The three pillars of good health are:

1) **The quality of elements consumed**
2) **Continuous detoxification and elimination**
3) **Proper exercise combined with ample rest**

Prevention is better than cure.

\- **Kamal Gandhi, MD**

Appetizers

Let food be thy medicine, thy medicine shall be thy food.
- Hippocrates

*baked sweet **potato fries***

- 3 medium peeled sweet potatoes cut into medium wedges
- 1 tbsp salt
- 2 tbsp black pepper
- 1 tsp coriander powder
- ½ tsp cumin powder
- 3 tbsp olive oil
- 2 tbsp chopped cilantro and mint to garnish

1. Place the cut potato wedges in cold water for one hour
2. Preheat oven to 450 degrees F. Oil a baking sheet.
3. Drain the fries and place in a bowl.
4. Add the oil, salt and some pepper and toss.
5. Spread evenly on the baking sheet, making sure there is space between them.
6. Bake for 10-15 minutes until crisp and golden.
7. Remove from oven and sprinkle with cumin, coriander powder and chopped cilantro and mint.
8. Serve hot with chilled mint cilantro chutney.

black bean tikkis

- 8 ounces black beans, roughly mashed
- 1 potato, boiled, peeled and mashed
- 1 red onion, chopped
- 4 cloves garlic, minced
- 4 tbsp chopped fresh mint
- 4 tbsp chopped fresh cilantro
- 1 tbsp black pepper
- 1 tbsp cumin powder
- 1-2 green chili, minced
- 1 tbsp grated ginger
- 1 tbsp toasted sesame seeds
- 1-2 tbsp salt
- 8-10 tbsp ghee for frying

1. Mix all ingredients in a bowl.
2. Make lime-size balls and flatten a little to shape the tikkis (about 10-15).
3. Warm a skillet on a medium flame. Gently shallow fry the patties with ghee a few at a time. Let each side brown (about two minutes) and then flip.
4. Serve warm with cilantro mint chutney and raita.

stuffed *jalapeños*

FILLING

- 4-6 medium sized jalapenos
- 2 grated potatoes (washed, boiled, dried, peeled, grated)
- 4 tbsp grated paneer (can substitute feta cheese or tofu)
- 4 tbsp chopped red onion (cut finely)
- 6 tbsp olive oil
- 2 tbsp cilantro
- 1 tbsp coriander powder
- 1 tsp cumin
- 1 tbsp dry mango powder
- 1 tbsp sesame seeds, slightly toasted
- 1 tbsp salt

BATTER

- 4 tbsp chickpea flour (besan)
- 1 tbsp paprika
- 6 tbsp water
- 1 pinch asafetida
- 1 tsp salt
- 1 tbsp yogurt
- 1 tsp turmeric

1. Mix all batter ingredients and beat well.
2. Make a vertical slit in the jalapenos.
3. Steam the jalapenos with ½ cup of water and 1 tsp salt in a flat pan until soft (3-8 minutes). Let cool.
4. Mix all the filling ingredients.
5. Gently stuff each jalapeno with 2 tbsp. filling.
6. Warm oil in a flat skillet. Dip the stuffed jalapenos in the batter and fry in oil until golden brown on both times.
7. Serve sprinkled with cilantro and mango powder.

spiced oven roasted eggplant

- 4 Italian eggplants
- 3 tbsp olive oil
- Salt to taste

- 2 tbsp coriander powder
- 2 tbsp paprika
- 1 tbsp chopped cilantro

1. Wash and dry the eggplants. Slice them in half length-wise.
2. Score the flesh deeply with a cross-hatch pattern. Be careful not to cut through the skin of the bottom.
3. Sprinkle salt on the pattern.
4. Keep aside for 20-30 minutes.
5. Heat oven to 400 degrees F.
6. Gently squeeze out the juice from the eggplants and pat dry with a paper towel.
7. Grease a baking sheet with olive oil. Lay the eggplant halves face-down.
8. Roast for 25-30 minutes until golden.
9. When cool, turn over. Mix spices and spread over eggplants. Serve hot.

mixed vegetable pakoras

FILLING

- 1 potato cut into thin slices (peeled)
- 1 eggplant cut into thin slices (unpeeled)
- 1 bell pepper cut into thin slices
- 1 red onion cut into thin slices
- 1 tbsp salt
- 2 cups avocado oil

BATTER

- 2 cups chickpea flour (besan)
- 2 tbsp yogurt (lowfat)
- 1 tsp. ajwain (carom seeds)
- 1 tsp. turmeric
- 1 ½ tsp salt
- ½ cup rice flour
- 2 tbsp cilantro chopped
- 2 tbsp mint minced

1. Place paper towels or a large plate or tray.
2. Salt the vegetable slices.
3. Warm the oil in a wok.
4. Mix the batter ingredients in a large bowl. Beat well.
5. Dip each vegetable slice in the batter.
6. Slowly lower each vegetable into the warmed oil. Fry a few slices at a time.
7. Flip after a few minutes until golden brown on each side.
8. Place on large plate/tray lined with paper towels.
9. Cool for five minutes and serve with chilled mint chutney.

spiced cashews

- 1 cup raw organic cashews
- 1 tbsp olive oil
- 1 tsp salt
- 1 tsp coriander powder
- ¼ tsp asafetida
- 1 tsp. black pepper powder
- 1 tsp mango powder
- 1 tsp paprika
- ½ tsp turmeric
- 3-6 curry leaves
- ½ tsp roasted cumin powder

1. Warm the olive oil on medium heat in a flat skillet.
2. Add the asafetida, the curry leaves and the cashews.
3. Keep stirring until the cashews are toasted, 4-5 minutes.
4. Add the salt and spices.
5. Keep stirring until well-mixed. Cool and serve.

*nachos with **black beans***

- 16 ounces corn or blue corn tortilla chips
- 16 ounces cooked black beans (drained)
- 16 ounces shredded Monterey Jack cheese
- 2 tbsp black olives
- 1 large red onion, chopped
- 1 large tomato, chopped
- ¼ cup, chopped cilantro
- ½ lime
- ½ avocado, sliced
- 2 green onions, chopped
- 2 tbsp pickled jalapenos
- 2 tbsp olive oil

1. Heat oven to 425 degrees F.
2. Coat a baking sheet with olive oil.
3. Spread a single layer of chips on the sheet.
4. Top with beans evenly. Layer the cheese, onions, tomatoes and olives.
5. Add another layer of cheese. Add sliced jalapenos. Bake until cheese melts, about 5 minutes.
6. Serve topped with cilantro and green onions.
7. Squeeze lime on top.

Chaat with Sprouted Moong

- 1 cup organic green whole moong beans
- 1 cup arugula leaves, washed and patted dry
- 2 stalks of green onion, chopped
- 1 chile, minced
- 1 tbsp salt

- ½ tsp turmeric
- ½ tsp black pepper powder
- 1 tsp coriander powder
- ½ tsp mango powder

1. Wash moong beans and soak overnight.
2. Drain and sprout in a flat colander, covered in a warm place for 8-12 hours (weather dependent—when colder, it will take longer for beans to sprout).
3. Mix all ingredients except the arugula in a bowl.
4. Toss and serve on a bed of arugula leaves.

pav bhaji

- 8 rectangular or square dinner rolls
- 6 organic potatoes, washed, boiled, peeled and mashed
- 1 cup cauliflower, finely chopped
- ½ cup green peas
- ½ cup carrots, chopped
- 1 large red onion peeled and chopped
- 2 large tomatoes peeled and chopped
- 2 tbsp cilantro leaves chopped
- ¼ cup bell pepper chopped
- 1 tsp black pepper
- 2 tsp cumin powder
- 1 tbsp mango powder or 1 tbsp lemon juice
- 1 tsp paprika
- 2 tsp olive oil or butter
- 4-6 cloves of garlic

1. Cook all the veggies (except for the potatoes) in a flat skillet with ½ cup water until they are soft on a medium flame
2. Melt the butter in a separate large skillet, add the spices and saute for one minute
3. Add the mashed potatoes and cooked veggies
4. Mash them all together
5. Add the salt and 1 cup water till everything is well mashed and blended together

TO SERVE:

1. Butter each dinner roll on both sides
2. Toast on a skillet and set aside
3. Serve by filling each roll with the veggie mixture
4. Garnish with onion, lemon wedge, and cilantro

potato tikkis

- 6 potatoes, boiled, peeled and mashed
- 1 red onion, peeled and minced
- 6-10 cashew pieces
- 1 tsp cumin
- 2 tbsp cilantro, chopped
- 2 tbsp mint leaves, chopped
- 2 tbsp pomegranate, fresh or frozen
- 2 tsp salt, or to taste
- 2 green chilis - optional
- 6-8 tbsp ghee or olive oil for shallow frying
- 2 tbsp bread crumbs

1. Save cilantro for garnishing. Mix rest of the ingredients in a bowl.
2. Make small, even-sized balls and flatten a little. Set aside.
3. Warm a flat skillet on medium heat.
4. Shallow fry a few tikkis at a time with ghee or oil till golden. Flip gently and serve warm. Best served with cilantro chutney and chana (garbanzo) curry.

falafel with cucumber and onion salad

FALAFEL

- 1 cup washed and drained cooked garbanzo beans (grind to a chunky paste with little water)
- ½ tsp cumin
- 6 cloves garlic peeled and minced
- 4 sprigs mint leaves washed and minced
- 2 tbsp washed and chopped cilantro
- 1 green chili, minced - optional
- 1 tsp salt or to taste
- 1 medium red onion chopped fine
- 6-8 tbsp ghee or olive oil
- 4 pita breads cut in half

CUCUMBER AND ONION SALAD

- 1 large cucumber peeled and cut in cubes
- 2 roma tomatoes or 4-5 cherry tomatoes cut in cubes
- 1 green chili minced
- 2 tbsp chopped cilantro
- 1 tbsp lemon juice
- 1 tbsp salt or to taste

1. Mix all falafel ingredients in a bowl.
2. Make 6-8 round balls.
3. Warm a skillet with ghee or oil and shallow fry a few at a time until golden.
4. Flatten lightly as they fry.
5. Mix salad ingredients in another bowl.
6. Serve hot with pita and the cucumber and onion salad.

kenia's papusas with side salad

PAPUSAS

- 2 cups corn flour masa (mixed with water to make a firm dough)
- 1 cup washed and cooked whole black beans (mashed)
- ½ cup grated mozzarella cheese
- 1 small grated zucchini
- 2 tbsp minced onions
- 2 tbsp cilantro, finely chopped
- 1 tbsp salt or to taste
- 4-6 tbsp olive oil

SIDE SALAD

- 2 cups mixed purple and green cabbage, finely shredded
- ½ carrot, peeled and grated
- ¼ beetroot, grated
- 1 medium red onion, chopped
- 1 tsp fresh oregano leaves or 1 tsp dry oregano
- 1 tbsp salt or to taste
- 1 tbsp lemon juice
- 1 green chili, chopped - optional
- 1 tbsp chopped cilantro

1. Make 6-8 balls from the dough.
2. Make a mixture of mashed beans, cheese, zucchini, onion, cilantro, and salt.
3. Heat a skillet.
4. Flatten a ball cupped in a palm of hand and stuff with filling in the center.
5. Fold up the edges and flatten gently in both hands until flat.
6. Cook on the skillet 1 at a time till brown on both sides.
7. Top with some olive oil after cooking.
8. Comibine all salad ingredients in a bowl.
9. Serve hot with side salad.

vada pav

VADAS

- 8 square dinner rolls
- 6 medium potatoes, washed, boiled and peeled
- 2 green chilis, minced
- 2 red onions, chopped
- 1 tbsp grated ginger
- 4-6 tbsp cilantro, chopped
- 2 tbsp mint, chopped
- 1 tbsp mustard seeds
- ¼ tsp asafetida
- 6-8 curry leaves
- 1 tsp olive oil
- 2 tbsp salt, or to taste

BATTER

- ¾ cups chickpea flour
- 2 tbsp rice flour
- ½ tsp turmeric
- 1 tbsp salt, or to taste
- 1 tbsp yogurt
- 1 tsp oil
- pinch of asafetida
- 2 cups mustard oil or unrefined avocado oil for frying

1. Mix all batter ingredients in a bowl and set aside.
2. Warm the olive oil in a skillet. Add the mustard seeds.
3. When it starts crackling, add the asafetida, curry leaves, ginger, garlic and chilis.
4. Add the onion and saute for 2-3 minutes. Add the potatoes, salt, turmeric, cilantro and mint.
5. Mix well and make 12-15 lime sized balls.
6. Heat oil in a frying pan on medium heat. Dip balls in batter and fry a few at a time until golden brown.
7. Cut dinner rolls in half and put a vada in the middle. Best served with cilantro chutney.

Salads

Part of the secret of success in life is to eat what you like and let the food fight it out inside.

- Mark Twain

baby spinach and berry salad

SALAD AND DRESSING

- 16 ounces baby spinach, washed and dried
- ½ cup strawberries, sliced
- ¼ cup whole blackberries
- 2 tbsp pecans or walnuts, chopped in halves
- 1 cup full fat plain greek yogurt
- 1 tbsp washed mint leaves
- 2 tbsp cilantro
- 1 tsp salt
- 1 tsp black pepper, or to taste

SPICED FETA

- 2 cups cumbled feta
- 1 tbsp ground cumin powder
- 1 tsp ground pepper
- 1 tsp ginger powder

CORN CHIPS

- 2 corn tortillas cut in thin strips
- olive oil for brushing

1. Add the spinach, strawberries, blackberries, pecans or walnuts in a bowl.
2. To make the dressing mix the yogurt, mint leaves, cilantro, salt and black pepper until smooth and creamy.
3. To make a side of spiced feta, mix all ingredients together.
4. As a topping, brush olive oil on the corn tortilla strips and bake at 300 degrees F until crisp and add to the spiced feta.

mixed cabbage salad

- 1 cup finely shredded purple cabbage
- ½ cup finely shredded green cabbage
- ¼ cup grated beetroot
- ½ cup peeled grated carrot
- 1 minced green chili
- 2 tbsp fresh oregano (or 1 tsp. dry)
- 1 small red onion, finely chopped
- 2 tbsp lemon juice
- 2 tbsp chopped cilantro
- 1 tbsp salt
- 1 tsp black pepper

1. Mix all the ingredients. Serve immediately.

sprouted whole moong and onion salad

- 1 cup whole green moong beans
- 1 red onion, cut into small pieces
- 1 green chili minced
- 1 tbsp lemon juice
- ½ tsp cumin powder
- 1 tbsp chopped cilantro leaves
- 1 tbsp grated carrot

1. Wash and soak green moong beans for 8-10 hours.
2. Drain and spread on a flat colander.
3. Cover and place in a warm place to sprout for 10-15 hours (weather dependent—longer when cold and less time when warm).
4. Once moong beans are sprouted, mix with all other ingredients and serve.

black bean and onion salad

- 1 cup cooked black beans, drained of water
- 1 medium onion, finely chopped
- 1 green chili, minced
- 8-10 cherry or plum tomatoes, halved
- ¼ cup chopped cucumber

- 1 tbsp chopped mint
- 1 tbsp chopped cilantro
- 2 tbsp pomegranate seeds
- Juice from half a lime
- 1 tsp black pepper

1. Mix all ingredients except cilantro in a large bowl.
2. Garnish with cilantro.

black chana with grated coconut

- 1 cup black chana (black whole beans) washed. Soak for 8 hours and cook until soft, for about one hour
- 2 tbsp olive oil
- 1 tsp. mustard seeds
- ¼ tsp asafetida
- 1 green chili, chopped
- 2 inch piece of ginger, grated
- 4 tbsp grated fresh coconut
- 2 tsp. salt
- 6-8 curry leaves
- 2 tbsp chopped cilantro
- 1 tbsp lemon juice

1. Warm oil in a skillet.
2. Add asafetida. Add the mustard seeds.
3. When they pop, add chile, curry leaves, grated ginger.
4. Add the cooked chana and salt.
5. Cook for 2-3 minutes stirring. Cool. Add coconut, lemon juice and cilantro and serve.

kamal's favorite salad

INGREDIENTS

- 1 cup arugula
- ½ red apple cut into 1 inch cubes
- 1 tbsp black currants
- 1 tsp feta cheese
- 1 tbsp pine nuts

DRESSING

- 1 tbsp lemon juice
- 1 tbsp extra virgin olive oil
- 1 tbsp crushed black pepper
- 1 tsp toasted cumin
- 1 tbsp orange juice

1. Mix all salad ingredients in a bowl.
2. Just before serving, toss the salad with dressing. Serve immediately.

*green lentil and **pomegranate salad***

- 1 cup french lentils, washed, cooked and drained
- ¼ cup pomegranate seeds (fresh or frozen)
- 1 medium red onion, chopped
- 1 tbsp cilantro leaves, chopped
- ½ tbsp salt
- ¼ tsp black pepper
- 1 tbsp lemon juice
- ¼ cup arugula leaves
- 4 washed and diced red radishes
- 2 romaine leaves, washed and dried

1. Mix all ingredients except the romaine leaves.
2. Serve on a bed of romaine leaves.

Vegetables, Dals, and Lentils

One cannot think well, love well, sleep well, if one has not dined well.

- Virginia Woolf

kale and sweet potato curry

- 1 large bunch curly kale, washed and finely chopped
- 1 cup spinach leaves, washed and finely chopped
- 1 large or 2 medium sweet potatoes
- 1 large red onion, chopped
- 1 large tomato, peeled and cut into small cubes
- 4 cloves garlic, finely chopped
- 2 tbsp olive oil

- 2 inch piece ginger, grated
- 1 tsp cumin
- 2 green chilis, minced
- 1 tbsp salt
- 1 tsp turmeric
- 1 tbsp coriander powder
- 1 tbsp lemon juice

1. Warm oil on medium heat.
2. Add cumin and fry until it sizzles.
3. Add ginger and garlic and fry for one minute.
4. Add the chili and onion and fry until translucent.
5. Add the potatoes and fry for 5-6 minutes.
6. Add the kale and spinach leaves. Mix well.
7. Add the tomatoes, salt and turmeric.
8. Cover and cook until sweet potatoes are very soft and combined with greens.
9. Serve garnished with coriander powder.

mixed vegetables in coconut gravy

INGREDIENTS

- 4 cups mixed vegetables (green squash, carrots, eggplant, red potatoes, broccoli, bell pepper) cut into small pieces
- 1 red onion, sliced
- 1 ½ tsp ground cumin
- 2 tbsp salt
- 2 tbsp coconut oil
- 1 lime, quartered
- 2 tbsp fresh chopped cilantro

FOR GRAVY

- 1 cup shredded coconut (fresh or frozen)
- 6 cloves garlic
- 2 inch piece of ginger
- 2 green chilis
- 1 tsp whole coriander seeds
- 2 tbsp mint leaves
- 1 cup water

1. Blend all gravy ingredients into a paste.
2. Warm oil in a skillet.
3. Add the cumin and fry until lightly brown.
4. Add the onions and sauté for 2-3 minutes.
5. Add the vegetables, salt and turmeric. Sauté for a few minutes.
6. Lower the heat and cover for 5-6 minutes.
7. When almost cooked, add the gravy.
8. Stir and cook for another 7-8 minutes.
9. Add hot water if too dry.
10. Serve garnished with cilantro and lime wedges.

cabbage curry with peas

- 2 cups finely shredded cabbage, washed and drained in a colander
- ½ cup frozen or fresh shelled green peas
- 1 medium tomato peeled and chopped
- 2 green chilis, chopped
- 1 tbsp grated ginger
- ½ tsp asafetida

- 1 ½ tsp turmeric
- 2 ½ tsp whole cumin seeds
- 2 tsp salt
- 2 tbsp olive oil
- 4 tbsp chopped cilantro leaves

1. Warm oil on medium heat in a flat skillet.
2. Add asafetida and cumin.
3. When cumin sizzles, add cabbage. Fry for a few minutes.
4. Add salt, turmeric, ginger, green chili. If using fresh, add peas now. Cook for a few minutes.
5. Add tomatoes, lower heat and cook covered for 5-6 minutes, until the cabbage is tender.
6. If using frozen peas, add now.
7. Serve warm, garnished with cilantro.

daikon radish and opo squash curry

- 2 cups washed, peeled and cut daikon radish in small cubes
- 1 cup washed peeled opo squash cut into small cubes
- 2 tsp grated ginger
- 1 tsp cumin
- 1 green chili, minced
- 2 tbsp chopped cilantro
- 1 tbsp coriander powder

- 1 tsp turmeric
- 1 tbsp salt
- 1 tsp black pepper
- 1 lime
- 1 tbsp olive oil
- 4 cups water

1. Warm oil on a medium flame in a skillet.
2. Add cumin and let sizzle.
3. Add the chili, ginger and sauté for one minute.
4. Add the radish and squash and sauté for a few minutes.
5. Add the water, salt, turmeric and coriander powder.
6. Cover and cook on low until radish and squash are soft.
7. Serve hot, garnished with cilantro and black pepper.

okra sautéed with onion and tomato

- 2 cups tender okra, washed, dried and cut into 1 inch pieces
- 2 medium red onions, peeled and chopped
- 2 medium tomatoes, cut into small pieces
- 1 tsp ground cumin
- 2 tsp coriander powder
- 1 tsp turmeric
- Pinch asafetida
- 2 tbsp olive oil
- 2 tbsp cilantro
- I tbsp salt
- 1 green chili, minced

1. Warm olive oil on medium heat in a flat skillet.
2. Add the asafetida and cumin.
3. When it sizzles, add the okra and sauté for 5-6 minutes, stirring gently.
4. Add the onions, tomatoes, salt, chili, and spices. Stir and lower the heat.
5. Cover and cook for 10-15 minutes.
6. Serve garnished with cilantro leaves.

taro root stir fry

- 5-6 taro root cut into long pieces, washed and soaked in water
- 1 tsp cumin seeds
- Pinch asafetida
- 1 medium red onion, chopped
- 2 tbsp chopped cilantro leaves
- Salt to taste

- 1-2 tbsp olive oil
- 1 tbsp mint leaves
- 1 tsp lemon juice
- 1 tsp paprika
- 1 green chili, chopped

1. Warm the olive oil in a flat skillet.
2. Add the asafetida and cumin.
3. Once it sizzles, add the taro root. Sauté for a few minutes.
4. Add the salt, spices and onion.
5. Cover and cook on a low flame for 10-15 minutes.
6. Serve hot garnished with green chili, cilantro and mint leaves and a dash of lemon juice.

cumin flavored pumpkin

- 2 cups peeled pumpkin cut into one inch cubes
- 2 tomatoes peeled and diced small
- 1 ½ tsp cumin seeds
- ¼ tsp asafetida
- ½ tsp turmeric
- 2 tsp coriander powder
- 2 tbsp chopped cilantro
- 1 tbsp chopped mint
- 2 tbsp olive oil
- Salt to taste
- 1 green chili, chopped

1. Warm the olive oil in a flat skillet on medium heat.
2. Add asafetida and cumin.
3. After it sizzles, add the pumpkin cubes. Sauté until translucent, about 2-3 minutes.
4. Add the tomatoes and minced green chili. Stir for about 2-3 minutes.
5. Lower the flame, cover and let cook for 5-8 minutes, until the pumpkin and tomatoes are well cooked.
6. Increase flame and add salt and turmeric. Sauté for a few minutes, mashing until well blended.
7. Serve hot, garnished with coriander powder and cilantro leaves.

basil and cilantro vegetable curry

INGREDIENTS

- 2 organic zucchinis cut into 2 inch pieces
- ½ red onion, sliced
- 1 carrot, cut into 2 inch pieces
- 2 potatoes, peeled and cut into 2 inch cubes
- 1 cup cauliflower florets
- 1 cup snap peas
- ¼ cup fresh green peas
- 1 chayote squash, peeled and cut into 2 inch pieces
- 1 tsp turmeric
- 2 tbsp salt
- 1 tsp mustard seeds
- 2 tbsp olive oil

FOR THE GRAVY

- ½ red onion, sliced coarsely
- 6 cloves garlic, peeled
- 4 small cardamom pods
- 2 cloves
- 2 inch piece ginger
- 2 inch piece cinnamon
- 2 bay leaves
- ½ tsp cumin seeds
- 1 tsp salt
- 4 stems fresh basil, washed
- ½ bunch washed cilantro
- 2 green chilis, chopped

1. Blend all gravy ingredients until smooth.
2. Wash and steam all the vegetables with salt and turmeric until almost cooked.
3. Warm oil in a skillet and add mustard seeds.
4. When the seeds crackle, add the gravy and the vegetables.
5. Serve hot, garnished with cilantro.

okra with mango powder

- 1 lb. okra
- 1 red onion, sliced
- 1 tsp cumin
- 1 tbsp coriander powder
- 1 tbsp mango powder

- 2 tbsp olive oil
- 2 tbsp chopped cilantro leaves
- 1 tsp turmeric
- 1 tbsp salt

1. Wash and dry the okra with a towel.
2. Trim the ends and quarter them lengthwise.
3. Warm the olive oil in a flat skillet on medium heat.
4. Add the cumin and fry for one minute.
5. When it sizzles, add the okra and fry for a few minutes.
6. Add the onion, salt and turmeric.
7. Mix well, cover and cook for 10-12 minutes.
8. Stir in mango powder and coriander.
9. Serve garnished with cilantro leaves.

*oven roasted **brussel sprouts***

- 1 lb. fresh brussel sprouts, washed, trimmed and halved
- 2 tbsp olive oil
- Salt to taste
- 1 tbsp black pepper
- 1 tbsp coriander powder
- 4 tbsp minced garlic

1. Preheat oven to 425 degrees F.
2. Mix brussel sprouts, olive oil, salt and pepper in a bowl.
3. Spread brussel sprouts in a single layer on a baking sheet.
4. After about 15 minutes, flip brussel sprouts over to other side and add minced garlic.
5. Roast until crispy on the outside and tender on the inside, about 25 minutes total, ten minutes after flipping.
6. Sprinkle with coriander powder and serve hot.

cauliflower and peas stir fry

- 2 cups cauliflower florets, washed and dried (1 medium sized cauliflower)
- 1 large red onion, chopped
- 2 medium tomatoes, cubed
- ½ cup peas (fresh shelled or frozen)
- 2 tsp grated ginger
- 6 cloves garlic, minced
- 1 tbsp turmeric
- 1 tsp cumin seeds
- 2 tbsp coriander powder
- 1 tbsp paprika
- 2 tsp salt
- 2-3 tbsp olive oil
- 4 tbsp chopped cilantro

1. Warm the olive oil in a flat skillet. Add cumin.
2. When it sizzles, add the cauliflower. Sauté until golden, 10-12 minutes.
3. Add the onions, garlic, ginger, tomatoes, peas, salt, and paprika. Sauté for a few minutes until mixed well.
4. Cover and cook on a low-medium flame for 5-6 minutes.
5. Serve hot, garnished with coriander powder and cilantro leaves.

*eggplant, potato, and **bell pepper curry***

- 2 medium red potatoes, peeled and cubed
- 1 medium bell pepper, chopped
- 1 long eggplant, cubed
- 2 tomatoes, peeled and cubed
- 2 tsp grated ginger
- 1 tsp cumin seeds

- ½ tsp turmeric
- 1 tsp coriander powder
- 1 tbsp salt
- 8 tbsp chopped cilantro leaves
- 4 tbsp olive oil

1. Heat oil in a flat skillet. Add cumin.
2. After it sizzles, add potatoes and sauté until translucent, 2-3 minutes.
3. Add the eggplant and bell pepper and sauté for 3-4 minutes.
4. Add ginger, tomatoes, turmeric and salt.
5. Add 2 cups of water, cover and cook until vegetables are well cooked, about 20 minutes.
6. Serve hot, sprinkled with coriander powder and cilantro leaves.

chana masala

- 2 cups garbanzo beans (chana) washed, cooked, drained; then set aside
- 2 medium onions peeled and chopped
- 4-6 cloves of garlic, peeled
- 1 inch piece of a cinnamon stick
- 2 small cardamoms
- 2 bay leaves
- 1 tsp toasted cumin powder
- 2 tsp salt or to taste
- 1 lime
- 2-3 tbsp olive oil

1. Warm the olive oil on medium heat.
2. Fry the onion pieces till golden.
3. Add garlic and sauté (2-3 minutes).
4. Add spices, stir, and set aside to cool.
5. Once cooled, blend to a paste with a little water.
6. Pour into a pan.
7. Add the cooked garbanzo beans and salt plus 1 cup of water.
8. Cook on low heat for 40-45 minutes and serve warm.

power greens with paneer

POWER GREENS

- 4 cups of mixed power greens (spinach, kale, swiss chard), washed and drained
- 1 tbsp ghee
- 1 tsp cumin
- 2 inch piece of ginger, peeled and chopped
- 1 tsp turmeric
- 2 tsp salt or to taste
- 2 tsp coriander powder
- 1 tsp black pepper powder (optional)
- 1 green chili (optional)
- Few onion pieces for garnish

PANEER

- 1 ½ cups ogranic whole milk
- Juice of one lime, freshly squeezed

PANEER

1. Boil the milk. When boiling, slowly add lemon juice 1 teaspoon at a time till it curdles and separates.
2. Cool and drain in a cheesecloth.
3. Gather the ends and squeeze out the water. Place a heavy weight on it to drain any additional water (10-15 minutes).
4. Cut into cubes.

POWER GREENS

1. Steam the greens with ginger, turmeric, salt and chili.
2. When cooled, blend.
3. Add the paneer cubes.
4. On a pan, warm ghee and fry the cumin.
5. Pour over the greens .
6. Garnish with cut onion rings and serve.

Rice, Grains, and Breads

*To keep the body in good health is a duty, otherwise we shall not
be able to keep our mind strong and clear.*
- Buddha

onion garlic rice

- 1 cup white organic white basmati rice
- 1 red onion, sliced
- 6 cloves of peeled garlic, chopped
- 1 tsp cumin seeds
- 2 tbsp of olive oil
- 2-3 whole black peppercorns
- Salt to taste, about 1-2 teaspoons
- 2 cups of water to cook rice
- 1 tbsp of cilantro for garnish

1. Wash the rice and soak for 20 minutes.
2. Warm the oil in a skillet or flat pan.
3. Add the cumin seeds and peppercorns.
4. When they sizzle, add the sliced onion pieces.
5. Sauté the onion pieces for 2 minutes.
6. Drain the rice and add to the oil with the garlic.
7. Sauté 2-3 more minutes gently.
8. Add the water and let it boil.
9. Add salt and lower the heat; cover and cook till done (about 15-20 minutes).
10. Garnish with cilantro before serving.

cardamon and lentil rice

- 1 cup white organic basmati rice
- ½ cup green french lentils
- 1 ½ tbsp olive oil
- 2 tbsp of cilantro leaves, chopped
- 1 red onion, sliced
- 2 bay leaves
- 1 tsp cumin
- 2 whole cardamom, slightly crushed
- 4-6 black peppercorns
- 2 whole cloves
- 1 ¼ cups water
- 1 tbsp of salt or to taste

1. Soak the lentils for 4-6 hours and cook till firm but cooked; drain and set aside .
2. Wash rice and soak for 30 minutes, then drain and set aside.
3. Warm the oil in a flat skillet.
4. Sizzle the cumin and then add peppercorns, cloves, bay leaves, cardamom.
5. Sauté for 1 minute.
6. Add the rice, the cooked lentil, onion and sauté till the mix begins to stick.
7. Add the water and let it boil.
8. Add salt.
9. Cover and cook for 10-12 minutes till dry on low heat.
10. Serve with garnished cilantro.

rice noodles with vegetables

- 1 cup rice noodles
- 2 tbsp of sesame oil
- ¼ cup sugar snap peas
- 1 ½ cup of green beans and carrots, cut into 2 inch medium strips
- 1 cup mushrooms, sliced
- ¼ cup broccoli florets
- 1 tsp mustard seeds
- 2 tsp minced ginger
- 1 cup green chili, minced (optional)
- 1 red onion, sliced thin
- 1 tsp salt
- 2 tbsp chopped cilantro
- 2 tbsp fresh lemon juice
- 1 tsp ghee or melted butter
- 2 tbsp of cashew pieces
- 1 cup water

1. On a flat pan, boil 1 cup of water.
2. Add the noodles and cook until they soften (2-3 minutes); drain and set aside.
3. Warm the sesame seed oil.
4. Add the mustard seeds and when they splatter, add the washed veggies, ginger, sliced onion.
5. Add salt and stir fry (2-3 minutes, don't overcook the veggies).
6. Join together with the noodles.
7. Warm ghee in a skillet and add the cashew pieces.
8. Add to the stir fry mix.
9. Garnish with cilantro and add lemon juice and serve.

ancient grain tortilla bake

- 2 organic ancient whole grain tortillas or any other tortilla
- 6 tbsp organic mozzarella cheese, shredded or more
- 4 stalks green onion, washed and cut small
- 1 green chili, minced (optional)
- ½ cup cooked black beans, drained
- 2 tbsp black olives
- 4 cherry tomatoes chopped into small pieces

- 2-3 tbsp cilantro leaves, washed and chopped
- Salt to taste
- 1 tsp of pepper
- 1 tbsp oregano leaves or 1 tsp dry oregano
- 1 jalapeno, sliced thin
- 1 tbsp olive oil

1. Heat the oven to 400 degrees F.
2. Grease the baking tray with olive oil.
3. Place one tortilla on the bottom.
4. Layer with a little bit of cheese, olives, onions, tomatoes, black beans, green chili.
5. Sprinkle with a little salt and oregano.
6. Place the second tortilla on top.
7. Spread the rest of the cheese on top of it.
8. Top with thinly sliced jalapeños and rest of the oregano
9. Bake for 10-12 minutes until the cheese bubbles and it has brown spots.
10. Garnish with cilantro.
11. Cut into squares and serve hot.

lemon rice spiced with whole red chilis

- 1 cup organic white basmati rice
- 1 tsp salt
- ½ tsp turmeric
- ¼ tsp asafetida
- 2 tbsp olive oil
- 1 tbsp mustard seeds
- 1 tbsp urad dal (small white lentils)
- 2 small pieces of ginger, peeled and grated
- 2 dry whole red chilis
- 3 tbsp whole raw peanuts
- 1 green chili, minced - optional
- 8-10 curry leaves
- 3-4 tbsp freshly squeezed lemon juice
- 2-3 tbsp fresh grated coconut
- 2-4 tbsp cilantro leaves, chopped

1. Wash and soak the rice for 30 minutes.
2. Cook rice with 4 cups water.
3. Add salt and turmeric to the rice.
4. Drain the excess water and cool
5. Warm oil in a skillet on medium heat
6. Add asafetida and mustard seeds.
7. When they begin to crackle, add the urad dal.
8. When the dal is golden brown, add the red chili and peanuts. Stir till peanuts are fried (1-2 minutes).
9. Add curry leaves, green chili, ginger, and sauté.
10. Add the rice, lemon juice, grated coconut.
11. Stir in the chopped cilantro and serve.

buckwheat flour rotis

- 2 cups buckwheat flour
- ½ cup chopped green spinach or kale
- 1 green chili, minced - optional
- 1 tbsp sesame seeds
- 1 tbsp salt
- ½ tsp pepper
- 1 tbsp mint leaves, chopped
- 2 tbsp cilantro leaves, chopped
- 3-4 tbsp ghee or olive oil

1. Set aside the ghee or olive oil.
2. Mix the rest of the ingredients in a bowl.
3. Make a firm dough, gradually adding water.
4. Add 1 tbsp ghee or olive oil to the dough and knead.
5. Make 4-5 even sized balls from the dough.
6. Warm flat skillet on medium flame.
7. Wet palms of the hand with water.
8. Take one ball at a time and flatten on the warm skillet with the wet palm.
9. Make a slightly thick, round roti.
10. Let it cook and flip to the other side.
11. When evenly brown, add one tsp ghee or olive oil and serve warm.

eggplant rice

- 1 cup organic basmati rice, wash and soak for 30 minutes
- 1 onion sliced
- 6 Japanese purple eggplants, cut into 2-3 inch pieces (then soak them in water to prevent discoloring)
- 1 tsp turmeric
- 1 tbsp salt
- 1 tbsp mustard seeds
- 2 tsp coriander powder
- 2 tbsp cashew pieces
- 6 tbsp olive oil
- 6-8 curry leaves
- 1 tsp paprika - optional
- 1 tsp black pepper
- 2 tbsp urad dal (small white lentils)
- 2-4 tbsp cilantro, chopped
- lemon juice to taste
- 4 tbsp fresh grated coconut

1. Cook rice with 4 cups water, salt, and 1 tsp turmeric. Drain excess water and cool.
2. Warm 2 tbsp oil in a skillet. Add the mustard seeds. When they crackle, add the urad dal till light brown.
3. Add cashew pieces and curry leaves. Set aside.
4. Warm 4 tbsp oil in another skillet. Add the onions, and sauté for 2 minutes.
5. Squeeze out the water from the eggplant pieces and add to the onions. Sauté till eggplant is cooked (about 8-10 minutes).
6. Add turmeric, coriander powder, pepper, paprika, and turmeric and let it cool.
7. When done, gently mix the rice with the eggplant mixture. Add coconut, cilantro, and lemon juice in the rice mixture. Serve hot.

black rice with cabbage and pearl onions

- 1 cup black rice, washed and soaked for 4-6 hours
- ¾ tsp salt, or to taste
- ½ cup pearl onions, steamed and peeled
- 1 tsp slivered almonds
- 1 tsp cumin

- 1 tsp ground black pepper
- 2 tbsp mixed micro greens or chopped cilantro leaves
- 4 tbsp grated green cabbage
- 1 tbsp olive oil
- ½ tbsp fresh lime juice

1. Boil 6 cups of water. Cook black rice for 40-45 minutes, covered on medium heat, until cooked. Add salt.
2. Drain water and set aside.
3. Warm olive oil on medium heat in a skillet.
4. Add cumin. When it crackles, add almonds. Sauté for one minute.
5. Add cabbage. Sauté for 2-3 minutes.
6. Add in the pearl onions, rice, and pepper.
7. Mix everything and add lime juice.
8. Garnish with micro greens or cilantro and serve.

cashew coconut rice

- 1 cup organic white basmati rice, wash and soak for 30 minutes
- 1 ½ cup unsweetened coconut milk
- 1 red onion, sliced
- 1 whole cardamom, crushed
- 2-4 whole black peppercorns
- 2 bay leaves
- 1 tsp cumin seeds
- 2 tbsp cashew pieces
- 1 cinnamon stick
- 1 tbsp olive oil
- 4-6 curry leaves
- 1 tsp salt, or to taste
- 2 tbsp cilantro, chopped

1. Warm oil on medium heat.
2. Add cumin, black pepper, bay leaves, and cashew pieces for 1-2 minutes.
3. Add sliced onion and sauté for 1 minute.
4. Add rice and mix for a few minutes.
5. Add coconut milk and salt. When it boils, lower the flame, cover and cook for 10-15 minutes.
6. Garnish with cilantro and serve.

couscous with mixed vegetables

- 1 cup couscous
- 1 cup mixed veggies, chopped fine (green beans, carrot, green peas, zucchini)
- 2 stocks of green onion, cut in small pieces
- 1 tsp cumin
- 1 tsp mustard seeds
- 6-8 curry leaves
- 2 tbsp of olive oil
- 1 tsp turmeric
- 2 small pieces of ginger, peeled and grated
- 1 tbsp of lemon juice
- 2 tbsp of cilantro leaves, chopped
- 1 tsp mint leaves, chopped
- 2 tbsp toasted almonds, slivered

1. Wash couscous in a tea strainer and soak in warm water for 10 minutes.
2. Drain the water. Warm oil on medium heat in a skillet.
3. Add mustard seeds. When they crackle, add the cumin, ginger, and curry leaves. Set aside.
4. Warm oil in a flat skillet. Add the mixed vegetables, turmeric, and salt. Cook for 4-5 minutes.
5. Add the couscous, green onions, and mint leaves.
6. Sprinkle lemon juice. Top with toasted, slivered almonds and serve.

Chutneys, Dips, and Spreads

The first wealth is health.
- Ralph Waldo Emerson

ghee (clarified butter)

- 1 pound organic cultured butter, unsalted

1. Melt butter in a pan on low - medium heat.
2. When melted, cook for 10-12 minutes, stirring constantly till golden yellow.
3. Use a strainer and pour mixture into a jar.
4. This makes about ½ - 1 pound of ghee for all cooking purposes.

*cilantro **mint chutney***

- 1 bunch of cilantro leaves with tender stems, washed and cleaned
- 1 bunch of mint leaves, washed and cleaned
- 2 pitted dates, washed
- 1 tsp fennel

- 1 ½ tsp salt (or to taste)
- 1 tbsp fresh squeezed lemon juice
- 4 cloves garlic (optional)

1. Use a blender to blend the ingredients and 1/2 cup of water into a smooth paste. Add more water to adjust consistency.
2. Serve with pakoras.

date and tamarind sweet chutney

- 4 medjool dates, pitted
- 2 small pieces of tamarind, seeds removed
- 2 tbsp black currants or raisins

- 1 tsp toasted, powdered cumin
- 1 tsp paprika

1. Boil the dates, tamarind, and currants or raisins till well cooked with 1 cup of water.
2. Blend to a smooth paste.
3. Add the cumin and paprika.
4. Add warm water until the mixture becomes a thick, sauce like texture.

spicy cilantro hummus

- 1 tsp paprika
- 1 tbsp olive oil
- 1 tbsp chopped parsley
- 2 cups garbanzo beans
- 2 green chilis
- 6 cloves garlic
- 2 tbsp extra virgin olive oil
- 2 tsp salt (or to taste)
- 1 tsp cumin
- 1 tsp cayenne pepper
- 6-8 mint leaves, washed
- ½ bunch cilantro, washed
- 6 tbsp fresh squeezed lemon juice

1. Wash garbanzo beans. Soak overnight. Drain.
2. Combine all ingredients in food processor.
3. Serve with whole grain pita toasted, crudité or crackers.

raita

- ½ cup whole milk yogurt
- salt (to taste)
- 2 tbsp grated cucumber
- black pepper (to taste)

1. Beat ½ cup yogurt.
2. Mix in cucumber.
3. Add salt and black pepper to taste.

green eggplant chutney

- 6 long green eggplants, chopped
- 1 red onion, chopped
- 6 cloves garlic, chopped
- 2 inch piece ginger, chopped
- 2 green chiles, chopped
- 1 dry red chili
- 4 tbsp chopped fresh cilantro
- 1 tbsp lemon juice
- 2 tbsp olive oil
- 2 tbsp grated fresh coconut
- 1 tsp cumin
- ½ tbsp mustard seeds
- 5-6 curry leaves

1. Warm 1 tbsp oil in a skillet on medium heat.
2. Add cumin and dry red chili.
3. Add the green chile, ginger and garlic and fry for 2-3 minutes.
4. Add eggplant and onion and fry for a few minutes.
5. Add salt and coconut and turn flame to low and cover until eggplant is fully cooked and mushy.
6. Mash well or blend with a little water. Stop when still chunky—do not liquefy.
7. Warm 1 tbsp of oil. Add mustard seeds until they crackle and then add curry leaves.
8. Pour over chutney and add lemon juice.

Desserts and Sweet Endings

A healthy outside starts from the inside.
- Robert Urich

shahi rolls

- 10 medjool dates, washed, pitted and chopped
- 6-8 figs, washed, pitted, and chopped
- ½ tsp cardamon powder
- 3-4 cups chopped nuts
- 2-4 strands of saffron
- 1 tsp ghee or melted butter
- 4 tbsp of powdered coconut

1. Warm ghee or butter in skillet on medium heat.
2. Fry nuts until golden.
3. Add dates and figs and cook for 3-4 minutes or until well mixed.
4. Add cardamom powder and saffron. Mix well and cook until the mixture forms a ball. Cool.
5. Roll the mixture into a log. Keep the coconut in a flat plate.
6. Roll the log over the coconut powder.
7. Tightly roll in a sheet of foil. Refrigerate for a few hours till firm.
8. Cut into 1/2 inch disks. Serve on a platter with nuts.

kheer (rice pudding)

- 4 cups milk
- ¼ cup white organic basmati rice
- ¼ - ½ cup sugar
- 2 tbsp chopped pistachios
- 2 tbsp almonds, slivered
- ½ tsp powdered cardamom
- 4-5 strands of saffron

1. Wash and soak rice for 2-3 hours and drain excess water.
2. Boil milk. Add the rice and boil and cover. Lower the heat and cook for 20-25 minutes.
3. Add the sugar, cardamom, and saffron.
4. Serve hot or cold. Garnish with almonds and pistachios.

coconut burfi

- 2 cups fresh coconut, grated
- 1 ½ cups sweetened condensed milk
- 1 tsp cardamom powder
- ½ cup almonds, chopped
- 2 tsp pistachios, sliced
- 2-3 tbsp ghee

1. Warm ghee in a skillet. Fry the grated coconut for 8-10 minutes.
2. Add some nuts and save the rest for garnishing.
3. Gradually add the condensed milk. Keep stirring till the mixture starts leaving the side of the pan.
4. Grease a plate with ghee and spread the mixture.
5. Sprinkle cardamom powder on top.
6. Let it cool and slice into several pieces and serve.

opo squash and saffron halwa

- 2 cups grated opo squash
- 1 cup sweetened condensed milk
- 4 tbsp ghee or melted butter
- 1 tsp cardamom powder
- 1 pinch of saffron
- 2 tbsps sliced almonds
- 1 tbsp pistachios, chopped
- 1 pinch of powdered nutmeg

1. Warm ghee in a skillet. Fry the squash for about 5 minutes until dry and translucent.
2. Add the cardamom and saffron.
3. Gradually add the condensed milk till well blended.
4. Stir for a few minutes until a ball is formed.
5. Garnish with sliced almonds and serve.

oats date *almond halwa*

- 1 cup steel cut organic oats
- ½ cup chopped dates
- ½ cup chopped almonds
- ½ tsp cardamom powder
- 4-5 strands of saffron
- a pinch of nutmeg and crushed black pepper
- 3 tbsp ghee or melted butter
- 2 cups water
- 1 tbsp slivered almonds

1. Warm ghee or butter. Toast the oats for about 5 minutes or until golden brown.
2. Add the almonds, cardamom, dates and fry for 2-3 minutes.
3. Add water, saffron, pepper and nutmeg.
4. Cook on a medium flame until dry. Serve hot, garnished with slivered almonds.

cream of wheat sheera

- 1 cup cream of wheat
- 2 cups water
- ¾ cups organic cane sugar
- ½ cup ghee or ¾ stick of unsalted butter

- 1 tsp cardamom powder
- 4-5 strands of saffron
- 1 tbsp slivered almonds

1. Warm ghee or melt the butter.
2. Add the cream of wheat and fry for 5-7 minutes or until golden brown.
3. Add water and stir till the mixture is dry.
4. Add the sugar, cardamom, saffron, and stir until completely mixed.
5. Serve warm, garnished with sliced almonds.

pumpkin halwa

- 2 cups fresh pumpkin, peeled and cubed
- ¾ - 1 cup cane sugar
- 2 tbsp ghee or butter
- ½ tsp cardamom powder
- ¼ tsp nutmeg powder - optional
- 1 cinnamon stick
- 6-8 strands of saffron
- 2 tbsp slivered almonds
- 2 tbsp chopped pistachios, raw

1. Warm the ghee in a skillet on medium heat.
2. Add the pumpkin cubes and saute for 5-8 minutes or till translucent.
3. Add the cardamom powder, sugar, saffron, and cinnamon stick. Saute till well mixed. Keep stirring for about 8-10 minutes, or almost dry.
4. Serve warm, sprinkled with nutmeg powder, almonds, and pistachios.

Smoothies and Drinks

You don't have to cook fancy or complicated masterpieces—just good food from fresh ingredients.

- Julia Child

*almond pistachio **date shake***

- 1 cup raw almonds, unsalted
- ½ cup raw pistachios
- 2 pitted medjool dates
- ½ tsp cardamom powder
- 4-5 strands of saffron
- 1 cup water
- 2-3 pieces of pistachio for garnishing

1. Soak almonds, pistachios, and dates in water for 3-4 hours.
2. Blend all ingredients till smooth. Add more water if necessary.
3. Garnish with pistachio pieces and serve. You can also serve chilled.

mango coconut smoothie

- 2 cups mango chunks, ripe and peeled
- ½ tsp cardamom powder
- 1 cup fresh coconut milk
- 1 pinch saffron

1. Blend all ingredients with one cup of water and serve chilled.

avovado and celery smoothie

- 1/2 carrot, peeled
- ½ avocado
- 2 celery stalks

- 1 cup of spinach and kale, mixed
- 1 red apple
- Lime juice to taste

1. Blend all ingredients except lime juice into a smoothie with 1 cup of water.
2. Chill or serve on ice. Add lime juice to taste.

beetroot carrot celery smoothie

- ½ fresh beetroot, peeled
- 2 carrots, peeled
- 2 celery stalks

- 1 cup of spinach and kale, mixed
- 1 red apple
- Lime juice to taste

1. Blend all ingredients except lime juice into a smoothie with 1 cup of water.
2. Chill or serve on ice. Add lime juice to taste.

beautifying **smoothie**

- 1 cup frozen dragonfruit
- 1 small frozen banana
- 1 handful power greens

- ½ cup strawberries
- ½ cup almond milk

1. Blend all ingredients. Serve immediately.

beetroot avocado celery smoothie

- 1 beetroot, washed and peeled
- 2 celery stalks
- ½ avocado
- 1 handful of power greens (kale, spinach, red chard)
- ½ cup wild blueberries (frozen)
- ½ banana
- 1 tsp lemon juice

1. Blend all ingredients into a smoothie with 1 cup of water and ice depending on how cold you want smoothie.
2. Chill or serve over ice.

banana berry smoothie

- 1 large banana
- ½ cup frozen organic wild blueberries
- 4-5 fresh or frozen strawberries

- 1 cup almond or regular milk
- 2-3 ice cubes - optional

1. Blend all the ingredients and serve immediately.

rose petal *almond milk*

- 1 cup organic raw almonds, soaked for 6-8 hours
- 4 cups spring water
- 1-2 dates, pitted

- 2-3 rose petals
- 1 tsp rose essence - optional

1. Peel and blend almonds and dates until smooth.
2. Strain in a cheesecloth and squeeze out the milk.
3. Serve decorated with rose petals.

notes

notes

notes

notes